Colors in Nature

Purple

by Heather Adamson

Bullfrog Books

Ideas for Parents and Teachers

Bullfrog Books let children practice reading informational text at the earliest reading levels. Repetition, familiar words, and photo labels support early readers.

Before Reading

- Discuss the cover photo. What does it tell them?
- Look at the picture glossary together. Read and discuss the words.

Read the Book

- "Walk" through the book and look at the photos. Let the child ask questions. Point out the photo labels.
- Read the book to the child, or have him or her read independently.

After Reading

- Prompt the child to think more. Ask: What purple things do you see outside? Are they natural or man-made?

Bullfrog Books are published by Jump!
5357 Penn Avenue South
Minneapolis, MN 55419
www.jumplibrary.com

Library of Congress Cataloging-in-Publication Data
Adamson, Heather, 1974-
 Purple / by Heather Adamson.
    pages cm -- (Bullfrog Books. Colors in Nature)
 Summary: "This photo-illustrated book for early readers tells about plants, animals, and rocks that are purple and how colors work in the natural world. Includes picture glossary"-- Provided by publisher.
  Includes bibliographical references and index.
  ISBN-13: 978-1-62031-041-0 (hardcover : alk. paper)
  ISBN-13: 978-1-62496-039-0 (ebook)
 1. Violet (Color)--Juvenile literature. 2. Color in nature--Juvenile literature. I. Title.
 QC495.5.A335 2014
 535.6--dc23   2012039682

Series Editor   Rebecca Glaser
Book Designer   Ellen Huber
Photo Researcher   Heather Dreisbach

Photo Credits: All photos by Shutterstock except: CanStock, 3; Corbis, 1; Dreamstime, cover; Getty Images, 10, 11, 13, 14, 23tr; iStockphoto, 7; Superstock, 8–9, 15, 18–19, 23tl, 23bl, 23br

Printed in the United States of America at Corporate Graphics in North Mankato, Minnesota.
4-2013 / PO 1003

10 9 8 7 6 5 4 3 2 1

Table of Contents

Looking for Purple

What things
are purple?
Look in nature!

I see a sea star.
Why is it purple?

barnacles

It eats barnacles!
Then it turns color.

I see a snail.
Why is it purple?

8

So it can hide.
It is hard to
see in water.

I see sand!

Why is
it purple?

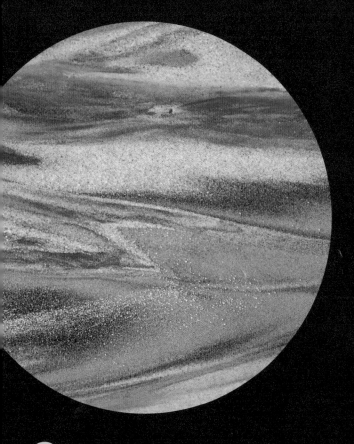

Waves crush purple rocks. They turn into sand.

I see a sea slug.

Why is it purple?

It's a warning!
A sea slug tastes bad.

I see a cactus.

Why is it purple?

It turns color when
it does not rain.

15

I see cabbage. Why is it purple?

It has nutrients. They are good for you. They make it purple.

I see a beetle.

Why is it purple?

It is hiding!

It has shiny skin.

It looks like dew
to other bugs.

Where do you see purple?

Shades of Purple

violet

lilac

plum

grape

Picture Glossary

beetle
An insect with a hard set of wings on top of a softer set of wings.

sea slug
A soft, colorful ocean animal with no shell and no gills.

cabbage
A large leafy vegetable; red cabbage has lots of vitamins, calcium, iron, and other healthy nutrients.

sea star
A sea animal with a flat body and 5 or more arms.

cactus
A spiny desert plant without leaves.

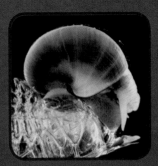

snail
A small animal with a soft, slimy body and a shell.

Index

To Learn More

Learning more is as easy as 1, 2, 3.

1) Go to www.factsurfer.com

2) Enter "purple" into the search box.

3) Click the "Surf" button to see a list of websites.

With factsurfer.com, finding more information is just a click away.